Fun, Fun, Fun!

by Susan Taylor

OXFORD
UNIVERSITY PRESS

We can sing and run. It will be fun.

We cannot wait.

She can sing a high song.
She sings and sings.

Dad hushes her. Then Dad sings a song!

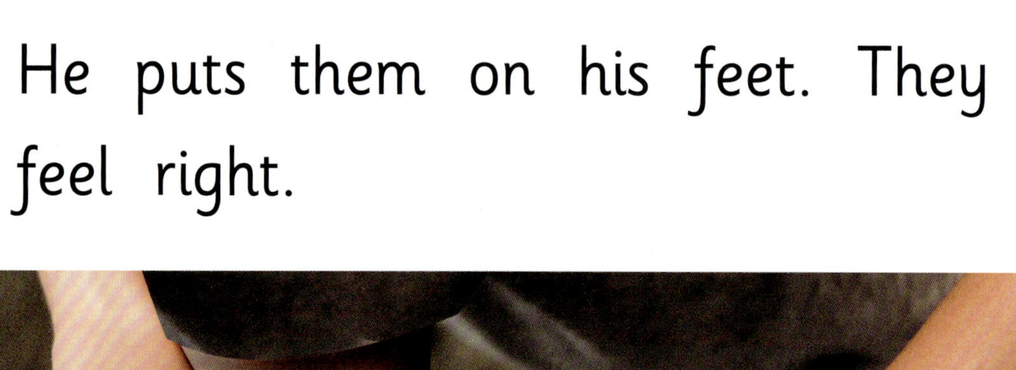

He puts them on his feet. They feel right.

He dashes along. He has quick feet!

Her coach pushes it to her.
She runs to it.

She kicks it right back. She puts it in the goal.

She has a pet dog. It has a coat.

She can run with her dog. It wags its tail.

He feels the rap. Then he taps his feet.

The heels on his feet go thud.
His feet keep tapping.

That was such fun!
thud bang

We can relax. We can belong.

Look Back

Encourage students to use the images to review the topic.